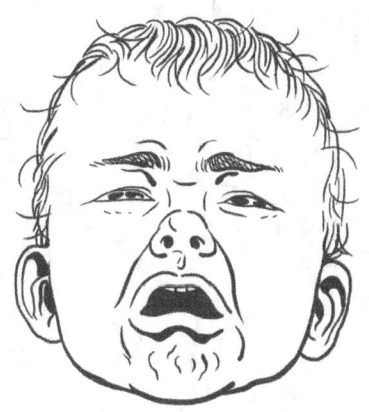

A riot,
    is the language of the unheard.

Martin Luther King, Jr.

Illustrations by
Tripuck Supawattana

Produced by
Chanasinj Sachdev

A Kraftka Coloring Book

"Riots"

Draw
your
Cause!

WORLD
PEACE

MArijuana
♡ 🍁 ♡

FLIP Page

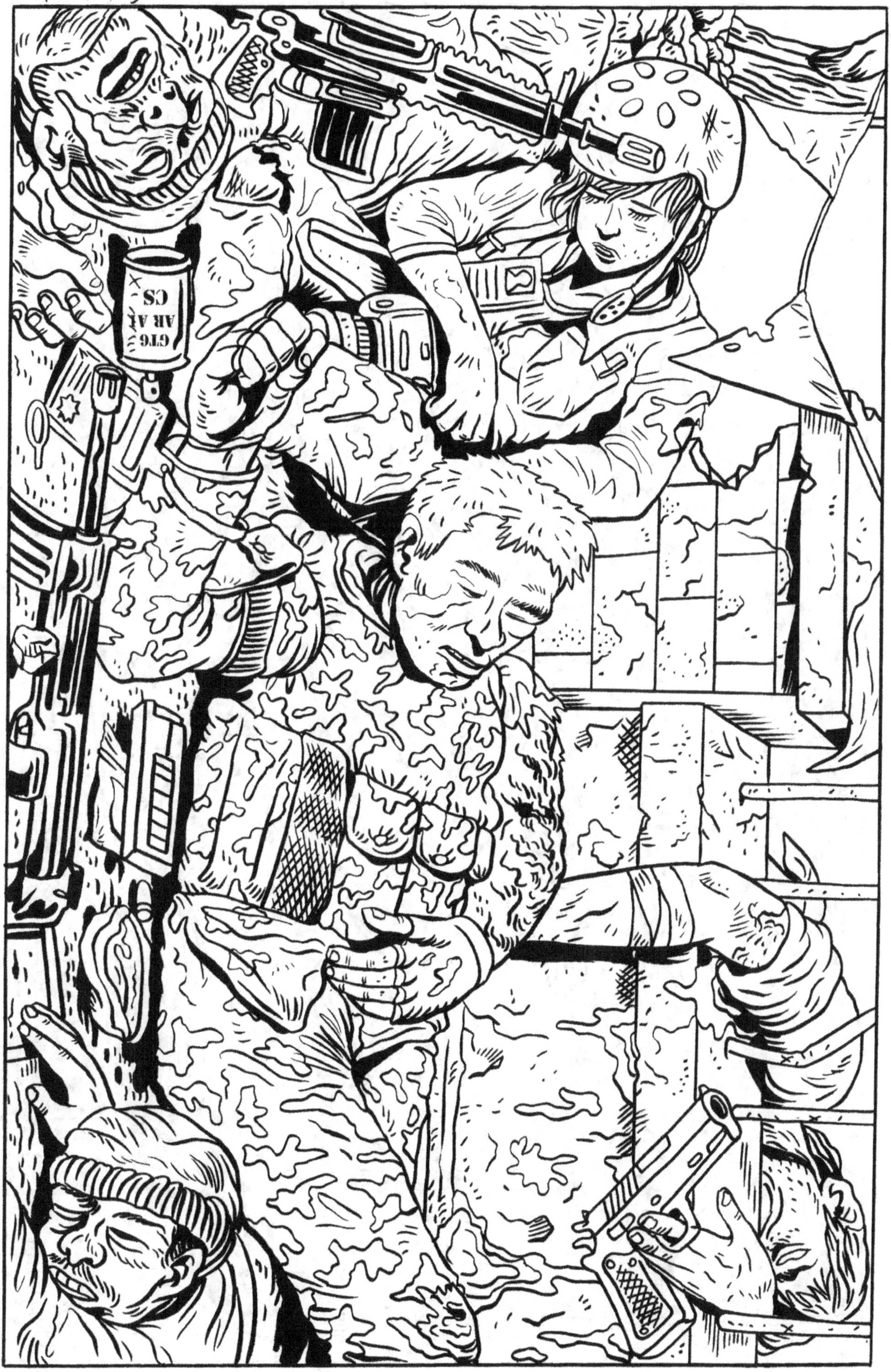

Draw your friends! your Flag

your favorite sports team LOGO!

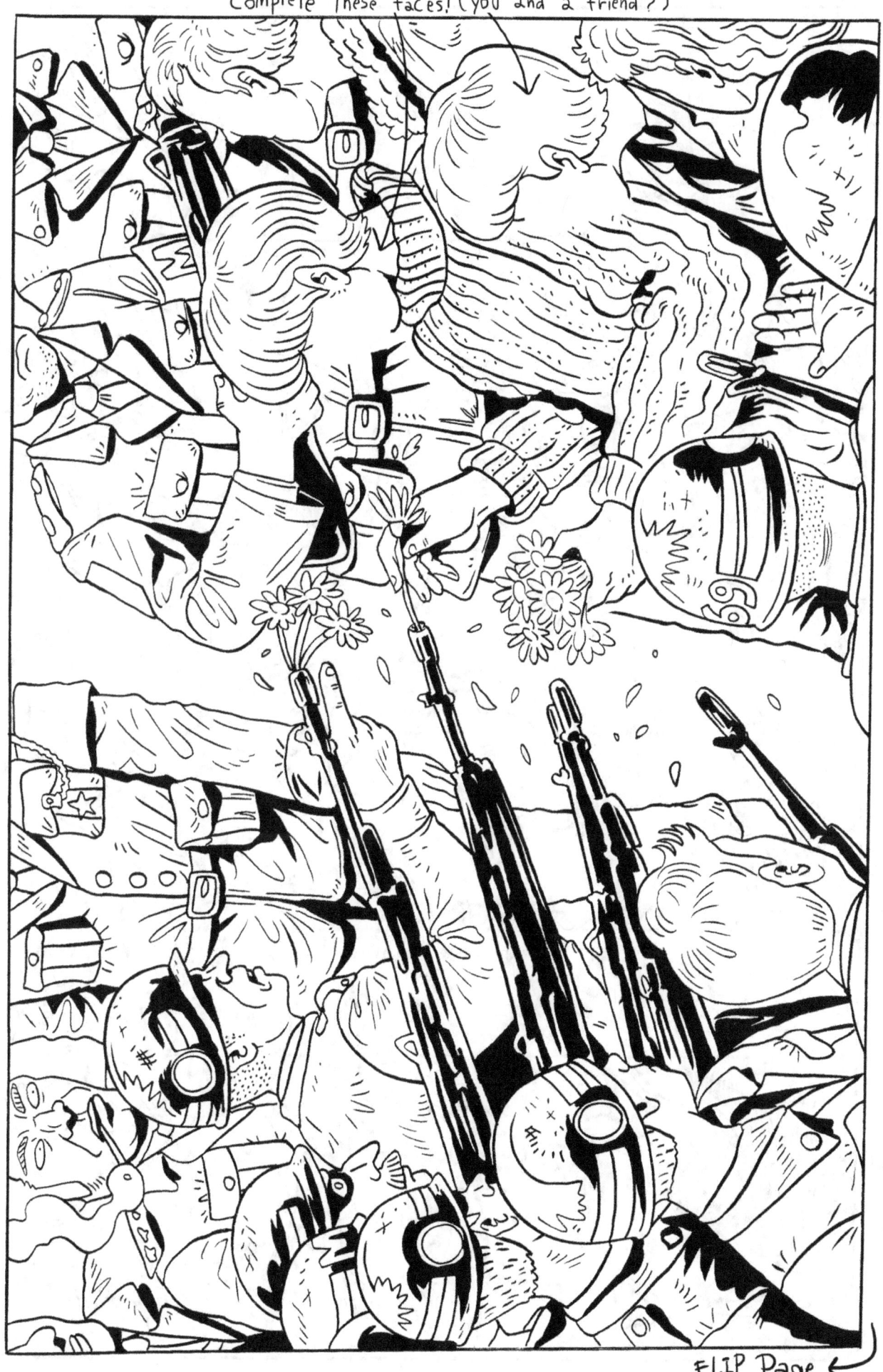

FLIP Page ←

complete
these
faces...
maybe
people
that
you know?

Draw your favorite band Logo

FLIP Page

Add a Cause you fight for!

your color determines the image — is she in front of bushes, or fire?

A photo of your loved One

What would you fight for?
Add your slogan.

FLIP
Page

What's he feeling? Draw his emotions.

THE END?

ABOUT THE ARTIST

Tripuck Supawattana or better known by his alias "Puck" is a Thai visual artist with a very distinct style that combines scathing social commentary and cartoonish charm. His work can be seen in innumerable comic books and fashion items, not to mention on walls all over Bangkok.

This book is a product of a collaboration with 'Kraftka', a new community-driven collective that aims to create unique pairings of artists and products globally to create compelling new experiences.